Lead the Way
After School

24 Leadership Lessons
for
After School Program Leaders

Paul G. Young, Ph.D.

Paul G. Young, Ph.D.

CreateSpace, An Amazon.com Company
Columbia, South Carolina
Available from Amazon.com and other retail outlets

ISBN: 9781728987743

Printed in the United States of America

To all the leaders who have committed themselves to establishing high-quality programs by learning and developing skills that will enable them to effectively create a vision and culture that enable children, youth, and adults to thrive.

CONTENTS

ACKNOWLEDGMENTS

My venture into the world of after school education has been two-fold. My first job in the 70s-80s was as a high school band director which required many hours of practice after the school day for various ensembles, especially marching band. As I reflect, those times working with young musicians beyond the school day proved to be a wonderful afterschool program, even though we never called it that. Now, research findings affirm that participation in extracurricular activities enables students to develop what developmental psychologists call *soft* skills, traits that are difficult to attain yet crucial for success. My students learned many music and performance competencies, but just as importantly they gained skills of self-discipline, grit, creativity, collaboration, growth mindset, and critical thinking.

Decades later, while serving in my final elementary school principalship, I was fortunate to play a key role in the development of an afterschool program created to provide needy students extra time to learn – after school – to complete homework, remediate and develop skills, and be provided with care and attention in a safe, nurturing environment. What started as a community volunteer program grew and developed into a 501(c)(3), model 21st Century Community Learning Center (21st CCLC) that continues to serve my former school community and other elementary and middle schools throughout the school district.

It is to all the hard working, dedicated individuals I've been fortunate to meet and work with through various local, state, and national professional networks that I am grateful for the leadership lessons they shared with me. These individuals are too numerous to mention or list here, but collectively they shared a common philosophy – *pay it forward*. That is my intention with this book. I hope emerging leaders everywhere will find the lessons contained within to be as helpful to them as I did when they were introduced to me.

The people associated with the afterschool programs in my hometown of Lancaster, Ohio – past, present, and future – will always hold a special place in my heart. I have tremendous appreciation for the ongoing support of my wife, Gertrude, and our daughters and sons-in-law, Katie and Jon Steele, and Mary Ellen and Eric Rahn, especially for their encouragement to write, train, and consult in a field that is very special to me. I hope my influence will, in turn, benefit professionals in afterschool programs who will someday care for my grandchildren, Nora and Evan Rahn, and Charlie and "Jack" (Jonathan Paul) Steele.

Paul G. Young
Lancaster, Ohio,
November 2018

Introduction

Afterschool program leadership matters! In an area of the educational continuum where research, professional work, and opportunities are greatly expanding, it is increasingly important to recruit, grow, and retain effective leaders. The need for effective afterschool program leaders has never been higher! Because of that need, an understanding of leadership theory, philosophy, and practice is greatly needed. Program directors, especially those new to site-level positions, must acquire knowledge, competencies, and essential standards of performance right away. For many, this important leadership role will be their first!

The purpose of this book, as well as *Lead the Way* (ExtendED Notes, 2014), is to provide aspiring and practicing afterschool program leaders with many of those essential, realistic, job-embedded lessons that will help them grow and thrive in their roles.

Description of the Book

Lead the Way After School provides short, self-guided overviews of leadership topics for which aspiring and practicing after school professionals must demonstrate proficiency to thrive in their roles. A companion to *Lead the Way*, this second book of lessons presents concepts with "how-to" strategies that can be used for quick, ready-to-go professional development training with after school program staff, laying a foundation for developing capacity and competencies that support adult job fulfillment, higher levels of student achievement, parent satisfaction, and program success.

1

Intended Audience(s)

It is anticipated that readers of this book would include, but not be limited to:

- site-level afterschool directors and aspiring leaders.
- afterschool program leaders (with overall program responsibilities).
- school principals and other school leaders who work with before and after school care programs.
- 21st CCLC program leaders, trainers, and consultants.
- early childhood program leaders.
- college and university instructors.
- professional association leaders.
- afterschool youth programs (YMCA, Boys & Girls Clubs, Parks & Recreation, etc.).

Why This Book Is Needed

This book's 24 leadership lessons are designed to support the training of emergent and newly identified leaders in the afterschool profession. Each lesson is a self-help introductory overview of a complex issue that requires months of study and practice to perfect. Adults are autonomous and self-directed learners. They have goals. They learn best when what they study and investigate is something that is relevant and applicable to their work. Most important, adult learners appreciate practical, hands-on learning experiences. That is what I hope to provide you as a reader of this book.

Along with introducing afterschool leadership lessons, I encourage readers to reach out and connect with others in the field and develop multiple layers of professional relationships and networks. Join and intentionally become active your state and national professional associations. Those organizations are designed to support the health and well-being of leaders.

Because people hold their leaders to high standards and the fulfillment of expectations is hard work, we need each other. Group learning supports the attainment of expectations. Reading this book, followed by a discussion of the leadership lessons with a peer group, will enhance your learning, help you achieve higher status, and secure your advancement in the field.

24 Leadership Lessons
for
After School Program Leaders

Paul G. Young, Ph.D.

Lesson 1

How to Survive in Your New Leadership Role

Now that you have been awarded your new leadership position, no matter whether you oversee just a handful of other people, or dozens, you must work to ensure that you survive and thrive during the first 120 days on the job. That's not an easy task because dynamics of human interactions permeate every work setting in differing ways and present unique challenges that you must skillfully address. You must deal with transition issues with your predecessor, your board (boss), your staff, the school(s) that your students attend, and numerous other stakeholders while creating your own identity and learning how to connect the dots with the political structures within your local, state, and national regulatory and support organizations. One of the first things you should do is join your state and national professional associations, get involved, make yourself known, and reach out for support. To survive and thrive, everyone needs supportive connections and a strong professional network. Don't become the Lone Ranger!

Acknowledge and Deal with Your Predecessor

Whether or not your predecessor was an exemplary leader, you must deal with the shadow that has been cast. If that individual packed his bags and left town, it might make your work easier, but in other ways the attention to your performance might be more intense. But if she was an exemplary leader, everything you do will be measured to that high standard. Regardless, it is best to develop a close, confidential relationship with that person (if possible), request advice, share your vision of the future, and seek support as you move forward. No matter how tempting, don't talk negatively about your predecessor.

Embrace Others' Memories of Your Predecessor

You'll be certain to hear, "But John did it this way!" sometime in the first 120 days of your tenure. Don't let that comment anger or undermine you. Transitions are hard. Leadership is often very lonely. Everyone needs affirmation and encouragement, especially those going through the transition with you. Acknowledge their fears and your predecessor's accomplishments and work to attain buy-in for your new ideas by building strong relationships. Don't whine or complain about what others have done or what you think you have inherited. Negative comments will always come back to haunt you. Talk about your predecessor like you hope people will talk about you when you leave.

Build a Relationship with Your Board or Governance Body

No matter whether your predecessor was effective or ineffective, you *do* need to know what caused others to form those opinions and why. But before you can engage in those sensitive conversations, you first must build relationships with key program stakeholders. Your credibility will be based on others' sense of your confidence, conviction, and competence. Once you have proven to be trustworthy, your board or governing body will provide support to move your vision forward.

Cultivate Your Own Vision

If your organization has a history of operating from an effective vision, it's good advice to embrace the goals set forth by your predecessor and work to move the targets forward. But you can't be your predecessor's keeper. Gradually, you must verbalize the organizational vision in your own words, clarify your direction and priorities, and lead with your own style. This is daunting yet important work. You must begin to emerge as a knowledgeable, competent leader within those first critical months on the job.

Set the Tone

People look to you for cues as to how they should interact, talk, dress, and work. If you fail to communicate the vision or take too much time to shape it the way you think is best, then you'll set a tone of inaction and confusion. People will lose their way and abandon faith in you. Their wish for "the way things were" will perpetually haunt you.

Take Care of Your Personal Needs

As you transition into your new leadership role, you'll work harder than ever before. Avoid jeopardizing your career by neglecting your personal safety, family, friends, and long-time professional relationships, or your financial security. Weaknesses in these areas will become your Achilles Heel, weaken your confidence, and limit your capacity to lead. Exercise. Read. Make time for yourself. And don't forget to check in regularly with those who are doing the same kind of work as you for mutual support.

> **The relationships that people form
> with afterschool program leaders
> are based on their perceptions of that individual's
> confidence, conviction, and competence.**
>
> **Leadership is lonely and sometimes dangerous.**
>
> **Where there is no conflict or pain,
> there is no momentum.**

Paul G. Young, Ph.D.

Lesson 2

Fundamentals of Leadership

Why should people follow you? It's a question that all afterschool program leaders should ask themselves. What is it that people need and want from their leader? Once you have been charged with the responsibility to lead, you'll quickly realize that motivating and persuading people to follow is challenging. Making hard, tough decisions is more difficult than what you might have thought it would be. Regardless, the leader must never lose sight of followers' needs and desires. Leadership is complex. To succeed, you must never lose your edge with the fundamentals. The self-reflective questions embedded in this lesson center around basic leadership competencies.

Competence

The questions people will ask themselves when they learn you'll become their leader will focus on whether they think you have the skills do the job. Are you knowledgeable? Can you demonstrate capacity to fulfill all requirements listed on the job description? Are you striving to increase your proficiencies? Do you ask questions? Are you a listener? Do you learn from mistakes? Can you communicate? People will size you up immediately as you display basic standards of leadership. First impressions are powerful. If they identify cracks, you'll forever be doing patchwork.

Integrity

Will you make the necessary, tough decisions even if it costs you personally? Will you confront those that are unethical? Do you demonstrate consistency in your actions, values, principles, methods, expectations, and measures? Most importantly, will you be honest and trustworthy when you are caught in an ethical squeeze?

Compassion

Will people know that you care? Will they see that you are willing to sacrifice for them as much as for yourself? Compassion is a virtue which incorporates a deep capacity to show empathy and sympathy. Are you capable of being socially interconnected with your followers, treat them humanely, suffer with them, yet still be tough when need be?

Courage

Do you possess the inner strength to confront conflict, fear, intimidation, and the unknown? Leadership is not only complex, it can be dangerous. Although there may be minimal physical threats or hardships leading an afterschool program, the challenges to your moral and social courage will be numerous. If you are not willing to stand at the front of the line and deal with what comes at you, people will not follow you.

Vision

There is nothing more frustrating and challenging for an afterschool program staff than to work for a leader who lacks vision. Managers cope with the immediate. Leaders deal with the future. Can you clearly articulate how adults and students in your program should interact? Can you describe program outcomes? Can you see how your actions, beliefs, values, and goals will be manifest in the overall vision for your program? The primary task of leadership is to communicate the vision and the values of an organization. That is done by articulating them in ways that support and reinforce their meaning. Visioning is an essential fundamental of any form of leadership, yet one that many leaders spend little time developing. It is very hard to get people to stretch and reach beyond themselves. It is nearly impossible to move people forward if the leader lacks competence, integrity, compassion, or courage to imagine the future.

Humility

The personal attribute that undergirds all the other fundamentals is humility. Does your ego ever get out of control? Do you become upset if someone takes your parking place? Do you cringe if you are not properly introduced? Would people say that you are arrogant? Obviously, leaders must have an ego - everyone does. And without a little bit of arrogance, people might ignore you. But the perception of humility is acquired over time. Keeping your arrogance in balance is important. Effective leaders know how to show concern and compassion for others, but they also must be able to like what they see in the mirror. The labor of self-love is a heavy one. Without humility, it becomes an unbearable burden.

What is it that People Need and Want from their Leader?

Once you are charged with the responsibility to lead, you'll quickly realize that motivating and persuading people to follow is challenging. Making hard, tough decisions is more difficult than what you might have thought it would be. People want to follow someone that they believe in, trust, shows consistency, cares about them, and is fun to be around.

Paul G. Young, Ph.D.

Lesson 3

Relationships Matter

The quality of an afterschool program is determined by the effectiveness of the leader's relationship with the staff, students, parents, school, and the community. Don't become so distracted and overcome by paperwork, to-do lists, email, projects, technology, and multitasking that you forget about the importance of relationships. Make relationship-building your priority, and your life and work will become much more enjoyable and meaningful.

Relationships Are Everything

That may seem like common sense, yet many afterschool program leaders choose to view their professional and private relationships separately. But the relationships you form at work are *personal* and they are *necessary*! Employees and program stakeholders who think you care about them will be be more loyal and productive than those who view you differently. One of the major determinants impacting staff turnover and program partnerships is the perceived quality of the relationship with the program leader.

Lead with Optimism

You can view your work and relationships with a doom and gloom and focus on the worst in people or you can select a more positive attitude. When you encourage optimism, your staff will follow your lead. You must believe in what you are doing and inspire others to do the same. Pessimism decreases performance. Negativity is contagious. Optimism lifts spirits and increases productivity. Leadership is the act of connecting and transferring your beliefs to others.

Build Trust

It takes years to build a reputation and only minutes to destroy it. You can't form effective relationships unless people trust you. They base their trust on the perception that respect is reciprocated, reactions are predictable, and the leader is typically prepared. Addressing people's sense of security is a key motivator in developing trusting relationships with them.

Spread Your Vision

People will not follow you until they believe you are worthy of their trust. They will follow *you* first, then *your* vision. When there is a force connecting the leader and staff, then you can clarify your vision, persuade and encourage people to work harder, and attain results.

Enhance Your Communication

Communication is the key to developing effective relationships. Uncertainty creates a void in communication and negativity fills that void. Relationships fall apart when there is a lack of communication. You must fill that vacuum with a variety of frequent and positive forms of communication that meets people needs. Don't forget to take time to talk with people, listen, and reassure them so that their fears won't breed and grow.

> Communication is the key to developing effective relationships. Speak from your heart and tell the truth. The simple act of saying thank you or using another form of expression of appreciation can make all the difference.
>
> **Gratitude is an attitude!**

Be Transparent

Speak from your heart and tell the truth. That seems like common sense, yet too often, leaders get sucked into their bureaucracies and become robotic in their dealings with staff over tough issues. Attempting to be politically correct will not always be the right course of action. Eliminate uncertainties and enhance two-way communication. People want to be led by those who share their emotions and have persevered through real challenges.

Reduce Busyness and Stress

Leaders with effective relationships figure out ways to reduce stress and balance their followers' personal and professional lives. They inspire, coach, and model the desired work ethic. The leader's positive energy makes the vision become a reality.

Fuel Your Passion

When the leader can show and give people purpose in their work, relationships will grow. Passion flows from purpose. When passion is fueled, it will take you to the next level. Relationships are everything.

Relationships are everything!

Paul G. Young, Ph.D.

Lesson 4

Leadership Truths

Leadership is about creating and driving change. If you lack the skills to build relationships first, you can't persuade people to follow. And if it becomes obvious that you don't know where you are going or have difficulty communicating a new vision, you can't effectively lead. Afterschool program site directors must be able to cast a vision of high quality, stir excitement, and unleash potential in students and adults.

A Title Doesn't Make a Leader

Just because you have an official title doesn't automatically make you a leader. First, you must demonstrate competence. Then, maybe, people will follow, but only if they develop a relationship with you. Leaders have influence. The most ineffective employee, a disgruntled parent, or the program bully can lead if they gain influence, either positive or negative, over others.

Academic Success Does Not Guarantee Leadership

There is no doubt that leaders need to have high levels of cognitive and emotional intelligence. Credentials are important, but they are not always an indicator of leadership abilities. In fact, academic excellence can sometimes produce an arrogance or elitist attitude that produces shortcomings and inhibits relationship building. Although it is preferable for afterschool program leaders to possess high-level academic credentials, there are many effective leaders who have never been to college.

Leadership and Management Aren't the Same

Leaders deal with people issues. Managers focus on processes. Many afterschool program staffs include competent members who excel with processes but lack the people skills and orientation to lead. Moving from process issues to people issues can be challenging and sometimes very devastating for those individuals who fail to acknowledge the different skill sets required of leaders. Effective program leaders understand others' conflict styles and cultivate relationships with people of divergent viewpoints. People don't automatically transition from manager to leader. It takes time, study, and trial and error rooted in reflection and skill development to learn how to become a leader.

Leaders Don't Motivate People to Follow

People become motivated to do the things that they find meaningful and fulfilling. They will follow leaders who provide an environment where they find that meaning. Leaders don't motivate with fear. They also recognize that pride is more powerful and meaningful than money. Motivation will be strong – and leaders will look good – where they inspire others with pride to be the best they can be.

Leadership Is Lonely

Leading people is complicated. Because human personalities are so varied, it requires high levels of emotional intelligence and empathy to build relationships. And those relationships must be based on respect, not friendship. Leaders become very isolated when they are faced with making tough, unpopular decisions. During extreme disagreements, leadership can be dangerous when naysayers personally attack the leader's actions and integrity. There is nothing soft about human behavior.

Leaders Rely on Intuition

Data doesn't always indicate a clear choice or path, and leaders must be able to make some important decisions without data. Sometimes, without really knowing why, you must trust your gut instincts and have the self-confidence to move forward. You also must have awareness of when you've made a mistake and reverse your direction.

Not Everyone Can Be a Leader

Strong leaders have big egos. But effective leaders know how to keep their big egos in check. They listen more than they speak. They remain open to new ideas. Effective leaders may possess some innate abilities that contribute to their success, but all leaders learn how to focus their energies on the job, strengthen their weaknesses, network, and connect with others who share similar levels of responsibility. Effective leaders are thick-skinned, accept getting knocked down, and know how to get back up. They have perseverance skills. They expect challenges and can take the heat.

> **LEADERSHIP IS ABOUT CREATING AND DRIVING CHANGE. THE LEADER'S JOB IS TO COMMUNICATE THE VISION FOR THE AFTERSCHOOL PROGRAM AND CREATE THE ENVIRONMENT THAT MAKES CHANGE HAPPEN.**

Paul G. Young, Ph.D.

Lesson 5

The Importance of Networking

Networking can be defined as any behavioral activity aimed at building, maintaining, and using informal relationships with others. Those relationships can be leveraged to acquire resources, advantages, and other benefits for both professional and personal advancement. Networking is important in both the public and private sectors. As the afterschool profession advances, it is essential that young afterschool leaders acquire an efficient and effective network with educators, policymakers, business and community leaders, and more.

Networks Should Be Intentionally Developed

Networking is important to everyone's career. Intentially-developed networks can influence earnings, promotions, evaluations, attitudes, and job satisfaction. The act of visibly networking brings you into contact with people that can share advice, provide key connections and introductions, and influence your insights about work in remarkable ways. Networking can heighten your power and influence. But if all you are really concerned about is expanding your list of contacts, your lack of passion for becoming part of a collective of professionals will be exposed. You must intentionally want to be a part of and contribuite to your professional community.

Networking Skills Can Be Learned

Intentional professional networking requires a commitment of time, thought, and planning. It is a continuous process. It also implies that you learn the value and importance of attending key functions where afterschool professionals gather. Before you go to those gatherings, make a list of the key people you want to meet whose connections could be helpful. Don't spend all of your time interacting with the same set of people you attend with and already know. Speak up and go out of your way to introduce yourself to new, diverse individuals in elevators, hallways, workshop sessions, workout facilities, shopping areas, or restaurants. Never eat alone. You will become known by the company you keep. Share your business cards during conversations. Return home with more cards than you left with.

Network with the Right People

It is also important to network with people in and out of the afterschool field. It is an optimal strategy to have a network that is diverse in numerous ways: socially, economically, politically, geographically, as well as including people of different race, creed and gender. It behooves us all to associate and network with high-status people.

Develop Both Weak Ties and Strong Ties

The time invested in networking, like anything, can become excessive. Therefore, differentiate between weaker, less formal but likely more numerous connections that can be used for new ideas and information, from stronger ties that will be better for further improving your existing knowledge and skills.

Dress First Class, Think First Class, Act First Class

When you choose to network, you want to put your best foot forward. That means you dress the part, act professionally, know the lay of the land, speak appropriately, ask questions, engage in dialogue, and commend the efforts of leaders when appropriate. Contribute to the good of the group.

Utilize Social Media

There are numerous ways to connect with your colleagues online. Facebook, Twitter, LinkedIn, and many other similar networks continue to expand methods to enhance your profile and professional memberships for added visibility. Building a network in a variety of media formats is very helpful. Contacts with different clusters or groups can position you to develop greater opportunities, learn and grow. Give, and you'll receive.

Get Involved and Contribute in Your Professional Association

Take your networking efforts to the next level by becoming involved in committees or serving as a board member of your state or national association. This work increases your visibility, provides you with access to new and "inside" ideas, enables you to influence decisions, and opens many new doors. Focus your attention on helping other people in your network. This produces goodwill and attracts others to your group. Networking is all about relationships. Build them and keep them strong. Working together is much easier than going it alone.

As the afterschool profession advances, it is essential that young leaders intentionally acquire an efficient and effective network with educators, policymakers, business and community leaders, and more.

Lesson 6

Mentoring Ethical After School Leaders

Everyone wants to work for an ethical leader. But what does that mean? Is it simply a matter of working for an individual that has the right moral values, a strong character, sets an example, and avoids the temptations and abuses of power? For most, ethical and moral values are synonymous terms. We follow and admire ethical leaders because of their virtuous values and skills, particularly trust, competence, and the perception of good intentions. If you are a new program leader, seek out a mentor. You can have more than one mentor. If you have experience and want to further expand your knowledge and skills, develop a mentoring partnership with a rookie. Together, you will learn more than either will alone.

Characteristics of Ethical Leaders

Many values are attributed to ethical leadership such as ambition, integrity, responsibility, accountability, respect, flexibility, and credibility. Followers also expect ethical leaders to be friendly, loyal, wise, generous, and optimistic. Ethical afterschool leaders not only talk a compelling and moral story, they live it by example. They are ordinary people living their lives striving to make the world a better place.

Live Your Values

As the leader, you must set the tone and establish performance standards for yourself, constantly keeping your actions above reproach. You can't lead and tell others how to behave if you don't live and act in accordance with the principles and values that have been established for the good of the organization. There are no exceptions.

Study and Prepare for Ethical Challenges

The most common ethical dilemmas contain power, authority, confidentiality, honesty and loyalty issues. While resolving these dilemmas, you and your staff will likely have different perspectives. As a professional development activity for your staff, talk through hypothetical ethical scenarios. Consider how you might deal with an employee that falsifies time sheets? Are copy machines available for personal use? Are gossiping and venting unethical behavior? Plan what you might do when facing other challenges and help others determine how they might best respond when they come up against an ethical dilemma.

Develop a Code of Ethics

A code of ethics establishes standards, rules, guidelines and values that govern and guide behavior. It also helps guide interactions among staff members and their work with the public. If your organization doesn't have a code of ethics, develop one. Use the National AfterSchool Association (NAA) Code of Ethics as a model and framework.[1]

Act with Selflessness

Ethical leaders focus on needs of others and consider how their decisions will impact them. They motivate others to put aside their personal interests for the good of the organization. They foster the exchange of experiences, diversity, ideas, and interests through all phases of the organization.

Maintain Impartiality

This doesn't mean you have to play the role of an umpire or a judge. Instead, it implies that you deliberate and make decisions based on impartial data and evidence based upon a standard set of rules for the organization and the profession. It also means that you take action to combat prejudice, discrimination, hate, and injustice.

Cast a Vision of the Future

[1] http://naaweb.org/images/NAACodeofEthics.pdf

Several factors will influence your ability to become both a visionary mentor and an ethical leader. You must have courage, self-confidence, empathy, and an ability to communicate effectively. You must be able to describe how, what, where, and when things will happen, and the way people should act. You must be persuasive, empowering, and able to display principled, trustworthy behavior through all endeavors.

You won't be viewed as an effective mentor if others perceive your actions to be cowardly, indifferent, biased, ignorant, or arrogant. Instead, your ethical leadership will be admired when people see courage, confidence, and commitment whenever you are weighing complex factors while, at the same time, working to treat people fairly and justly.

> Knowing the right thing to do is critical
> in personal and professional ethics.
> Yet, ethics only happens when good beliefs
> lead to good behaviors.
> Without the action part,
> all you have are good intentions.

Ethical Scenarios

The scenarios on this page are provided for personal self-reflection or usage between mentors and mentees.

What Can, and Should You Do?

#1. The school(s) your students attend has a Reading Recovery Program for struggling students that in your opinion leaves a lot to be desired. You have observed students attending your afterschool program sitting in front of a computer doing exercise after exercise with little or no teacher support. The principal believes in this program and expects his teaching staff, you, and your program staff to be supportive and extend the interventions in similar ways after school. Meanwhile, you know these struggling students are falling farther behind. What can, and should you do?

#2. The school principal calls you to inform you that a parent has called her complaining about the demeanor of one your program staff members. The principal never tells who the parent is—although the principal did say that the parent has a long history and good reputation with teachers at her school. You have no reason to suspect any improper behavior of any of your staff members, even the one being signaled out. The principal seemed to take this parent's word as gold. What can, and should you do?

#3. Your contract with afterschool staff states the program hours run from 3:00 to 6:00 p.m. Monday thru Friday. Staff are also paid for 30 minutes of planning and preparation (without students) starting at 2:30. One of your staff members arrives at 2:40 p.m. as often as three days per week, but her sign-in sheet states she always arrives by 2:30. What can, and should you do?

#4. Office supplies which belong to the school (your program is housed in a public school), such as reams of paper, plastic thumbtacks, paper clips, pens and pencils, and folders, are taken home by one of your program staff members for personal use. What can, and should you do?

Lesson 7

Managing Gen-Zers, Millennials, Gen-Xers, Boomers, and Workers of All Ages

Afterschool program directors in their 40s or older often voice concerns about challenges they encounter working with younger, twenty-something employees, who were born in the 80s, 90s, or after 2000. A decade or more ago, it was common to complain about Generation Y (or the Millennials) - 78 million of them who were then relatively new to the workforce. But now, it is the emergence of Generation Z, born mostly after 1997, who are entering college and the workforce. The work of recruiting, retaining, and motivating people of each generation differs greatly.

Common complaints about millennials focused on their infatuation with cell phones, texting, and the Internet. They often showed up at work wearing flip flops, earrings, and headphones. They'd been reared in structured and sheltered homes by doting parents. They showed respect and tolerance for diversity. They entered the workforce seeking flexibility and responsibility in ways that often created conflict with their more veteran co-workers. What follows are strategies that afterschool program directors can utilize to manage them, and other young workers, effectively.

Provide Structure

The millennials' parents structured and scheduled their lives around their kids' sports, music, and other extracurricular and afterschool activities. As a result, it's natural for millennials to cram their lives with multiple activities, including lots of time with family and friends. They will work hard, but not the extensive hours of the Baby Boomers. Balance and multiple activities are important to young workers. Provide clarity around assignments, due dates, goals, meeting agendas, and required work hours.

Keep Them Informed

How afterschool leaders communicate and send messages may not be understood by Millennials and Gen-Zers. They may not focus on what you say. They may need messages conveyed in text or another format. If there is ambiguity about objectives and expectations, trust will be eroded. If you feel you aren't being heard, try adapting by using a medium preferred by the younger generation.

Listen to Them

The millennials have always been encouraged to express their ideas and opinions. As a result, they don't like having their thoughts ignored. But their thoughts are often conveyed using text messaging, Facebook, Twitter, and other means of communication less used by older managers. To listen effectively, afterschool leaders must learn to fully utilize the millennials' and Gen-Zers' communication tools.

Don't Bore Them

Millennials and Gen-Zers appreciate changing tasks at work. Don't bore them, ignore them, or trivialize their contribution. Multiple tasks don't bother them. They've grown up being allowed to multitask. Despite the drawbacks to multitasking, this generational characteristic must be acknowledged. Without constant challenges and change, young workers will likely experience boredom.

Tap into Their Strengths

Younger workers' electronic capabilities are one of their most defining characteristics. Provide them the challenge of establishing communications and networking with people in other countries. Let them create and teach using technology. They are comfortable working in teams and interacting with diverse groups on a wide range of social topics. They will excel leading global and blended learning initiatives where they have the freedom to mix different learning goals, particularly with the technology-based activities.

Make Work Fun

The millennials and Gen-Zers want to enjoy their work and make friends in the work setting. Create an environment where there is laughter, group sharing, acknowledgement of effort, and social networking after work hours. Develop team building activities that enable workers with different generational characteristics to work side-by-side and develop mutual interests and respect. Help young workers learn why their work is important by teaching the purpose and articulating the value of varied tasks. Thet want to look up to you, learn from you, and receive daily feedback. They want to be included and kept in the know. Teach, coach, and mentor them. Acknowledge differences. An investment of time will result in their success and happiness - afterschool.

> Young people entering the afterschool workforce have grown up in a digitized environment with cell phones, the Internet, texting, social media networking, and more. To engage them and help them become productive workers, afterschool leaders must capitalize on the contributions they are best prepared to make, rather than villainize them.

Lesson 8

Instilling a Work Ethic in the Emerging After School Workforce

Have you ever been asked to write a letter of recommendation for an employee or co-worker yet privately had reservations? You think he should know the right things to do, but he fails to do anything adequately. Even though she possesses some admiral skills, she lacks the core values of a positive work ethic that every employer hopes to find when interviewing and hiring. If you've been in that situation, or if you feel that, in general, your staff's work ethic needs improvement, it is advisable to take time to talk about, teach, and clarify the specifics of what you expect from every employee. Use the topics that follow in this leadership lesson as guide for developing "teaching conversations" about work ethic values.

Professionalism

Professionalism implies that you look and act your best. Afterschool professionals value fashion and proper appearance, including attire, hair styling, hygiene, and use of makeup. Knowing how to dress for success is just as important to be demonstrated by those in hourly, frontline staff positions as it is by the boss. Professionals display manners, courtesy, and use language appropriately. Clarity and adherance to the program's dress code is crucial to development of professionalism.

Attitude

It's simple. Those with a good work ethic smile and play nice. They show gratitude. They're polite. They say please and thank you. An attitude is an outward display of internal views. It's where perceptions become realities. Those with a positive attitude should mentor new hires. Positive attitudes can be contagious. Develop a checklist of observable positive attitude attributes (see Table 8.1, p. 36). Teach them to your staff.

Reliability

It's hard to write a recommendation for tardy, unreliable employees. Nothing is more basic or foundational to a good work ethic than reliability. Yet, too many people have become accustomed to making excuses. For too many people, reliability is becoming a "yeah but" value. Program leaders shouldn't wait for infractions to occur. Teach your expectations of punctuality, dependability, and self-responsibility. Those who master the value of reliability will always be in high demand!

Initiative

Initiative requires ambition. Strive to do your best and accomplish more than is expected. Model this value and others will emulate it. If you can specifically write about how an employee exhibited pride and passion in every work task, it will catch the eye of potential employers. Those with initiative don't settle for minimum standards. They soar beyond.

Respect

To gain respect, play by the rules and teach employees to do the same. Respect implies being able to show obedience, acceptance, and conformity. Workers must respect their peers, managers, students, parents, and the parameters of their contract. The development of mentoring partnerships can greatly impact efforts to instill respect into an organization.

Integrity

Employers seek workers that are honest and speak the truth. Integrity must be the foundation of every afterschool program and part of every code of conduct. There is no place for dysfunctional or antisocial individuals in the afterschool workforce.

Competence

Every job requires a specified level of requisite knowledge and competence. Those who willingly read and engage in professional development because they want to learn and continuously improve gain the highest levels of recognition. Those individuals who demonstrate the habits and ideals of a positive work ethic need never worry about a performance review. Nor will they need worry about what a supervisor will write in a recommendation. The description of their work ethic will say enough!

> **Afterschool employers want candidates who are positive, dependable, dedicated, honest, coachable, well-groomed, and who go out of their way to add value to the program and do more than what's expected of them.**
>
> **Simply put, they want candidates with a positive work ethic.**

Table 8. 1 - Checklist of Positive Attitude and Work Ethic Attributes
(Keep this list handy when interviewing potential job candidates)

	Attribute	Yes	No
1.	Maintains positive **eye contact** when conversing.		
2.	Speaks with **clarity and accuracy.**		
3.	Employs positive **clicking skills** when meeting people.		
4.	Displays a **smile and positive body language.**		
5.	Shows **gratitude** toward others.		
6.	Demonstrates **self-motivation.**		
6.	Possesses a **growth mindset** vs. a fixed mindset.		
7.	Displays **perseverance** in challenging situations.		
8.	Shows **cooperative, collaborative** work habits.		
9.	Consistently follows through – **dependable.**		
10.	Focusing on **giving** more than receiving.		
11.	Presents solutions; capable **problem-solver.**		
12.	Displays **integrity** by making good choices.		
13.	Shows **reliability** by doing what he says he will do when he says he will do it.		
14.	Always on time, **punctual.**		
15.	**Organized** and **prepared.**		
16.	**Empathetic** toward needs and desires of others.		
17.	**Dedicated** to the task at hand.		
18.	Shows **initiative** and has a history of **productivity.**		
19.	Possesses an **optimistic view of failure.**		
20.	Asks good questions, **curious.**		
21.	Has a pattern habits of **continuous learning.**		
22.	Easily acknowledges and **celebrates others' success.**		
23.	Understands the **value of diversity and inclusion.**		
24.	Displays **common sense.**		
25.	Practices **professionalism.**		

Lesson 9

Instilling the Virtues of
Grit and Growth Mindset

What is a Growth Mindset? Stanford psychologist Carol Dweck describes it as a person's general attitude or predisposition about the way they think about things. A person's mindset is malleable and will grow and change. Kids with a growth mindset think they can learn anything. Those with fixed mindsets tend to shy away from challenges and quit when things get difficult (Dweck, 2007).

What is Grit? It's what makes high achievers special. According to psychologist Angela Duckworth, who has researched the concept and coined the term grit, it is passion and perseverance for accomplishing long term goals, described as a "protective coating" against the negative effects of stress in school and at home (Duckworth, 2016).

Why are These Important Skills for Kids?

An overarching goal of parenting is rearing kids to be able to create their own future. They will use their beliefs, values, and reference frames to organize their world, establish goals, stick with them, and never give up.

How Can Grit and Mindset Be Taught?

Practitioners are developing classroom and parenting strategies, but perhaps the most effective method is to model the skills in one-to-one or small group mentoring partnerships. Kids need to learn grit and mindset vocabulary, identify key people in their lives who demonstrate the skills, and interact with and be encouraged by gritty adults in school and at home. Multi-year participation in extra-curricular activities is an excellent way to learn and acquire grit and growth mindset skills.

What Grit Skills Can Be Learned from Extra-curricular Participation?

Kids who are coached learn to take constructive criticism in any form and to learn and grow from it. Coachable players want to improve for their own good as well as their team. Coaching produces self-discipline, better physical health, higher academic achievement, less behavioral problems, perseverance in college, success in employment, and higher lifetime earnings.

Together, What Can Parents and Teachers Do?

Rethink school and home-based practices that have led to an undesirable sense of entitlement among too many children and youth. As children progress through elementary grades, discuss when it is appropriate for each child to assume autonomous responsibility for their homework, grades, social interactions, fighting personal battles, and completing chores. By planning, sharing strategies, and developing a close working partnership, children with fixed mindset tendencies will not be able to drive wedges between you. Don't micromanage every aspect of children's lives. Most importantly, praise effort rather than the achievement of high grades. Ensure that kids learn the importance of trying – not crying.

> **Students who have grit and characteristics of a growth mindset can put a positive spin on negative experiences. They learn from their mistakes and gain benefits from "good failures."**

Without a doubt, there are many challenges in raising and educating children. To help kids survive and thrive as young adults, we must look beyond efforts in reading, writing, math, and demonstrating proficiency in other content areas, and work together to teach and model important character skills, particularly grit and growth mindset, which a growing body of research says may matter more to overall success in life than native intelligence.

Available from Amazon.com and other retail outlets.

This book is a commonsense resource for busy afterschool program leaders and their staffs who face the challenges of helping kids increase their perseverance and develop the mindset and motivation to complete homework and fully engage in out-of-school learning experiences. The book is packed full of ready-to-use professional development, resources, trips, vignettes, and instructional activities.

Paul G. Young, Ph.D.

Lesson 10

The Power of Deliberate Practice

If you want to become a better afterschool program leader, you'll have to practice. You've likely been told this many times before when you've contemplated getting better at anything you've wanted to do. Similarly, a major emphasis of afterschool programs should be to motivate and teach kids to get better through practice. We must be their role models. Recent studies are showing that to achieve at the elite status of anything – sports, music, science, chess, public speaking, leadership, whatever – requires 10,000 hours of deliberate practice (Gladwell, 2008). At 20 hours a week, that takes 10 years. No doubt, anyone with 10 years of experience leading afterschool programs is likely going to have improved their skills to some degree, but those who put forth effort toward developing the *quality* of their practice rather than just accumulating a *quantity* of practice hours rise to brilliance while others reach a plateau that is just good.

Define Deliberate Practice

Many people with 30 years of experience in a job really have one year of experience that they've repeated 29 times. You know them. They are nice, hardworking people, but sometimes not very sharp on the job. Those who set out to deliberately improve their leadership skills know they must repeatedly engage in overcoming the challenges, tasks, and activities that are most difficult. They have focus. They don't proscrastinate. They accept constructive feedback. They dellberately practice the most difficult skills and improve performance until they become automatic.

Deliberately Practice While Doing Your Job

The most difficult work for afterschool leaders might be visioning, strategizing, persuading and guiding people, and engaging in various forms of big picture thinking. It is likely not the tasks of managing paperwork, schedules, students, or parents. On top of the essential administrative tasks you have to complete, you still have to find time to deliberately practice the difficult skills essential for elite performance. Even if you don't get to the 10,000-hour mark, deliberately practicing the toughest leadership skills will make you better and prepare you for your *next* job. Start small. Strive to find at least one hour each day to practice a skill at which you want to excel that stretches you.

Seek Constructive Feedback

To master the stressful stretch skills and move beyond your comfort zone, you need to seek guidance and feedback from a mentor, coach, critical friend, coworker, or anyone you trust to provide a good critique of your performance. Assess how well you are doing and what you can do specifically to improve. Gradually increase the pace of your efforts. When you get used to perfecting the tough tasks, your stress level will decrease, and you will enjoy the work. The hardest part is asking for help.

Compete Against Yourself, Not Others

Don't compare yourself to what you see others doing. What matters most today is getting better than you were yesterday. Elite pianists know that they must practice and master the most difficult technical aspects of the few measures of complex works that separate good from elite players. They break them down and practice them over and over until they become easy and automatic. They have only themselves to blame for mistakes. They respect and celebrate with colleagues who have accomplished these tough goals.

Do Your Best in the Present

It is important to plan and set long-term goals, but you also must be able to perform in the present. To succeed at Weight Watchers, you must follow the plan and resist the urges to stray and splurge when they inevitably appear. When you pay forward with deliberate practice, the rewards are sure to follow. Focus on details that you can fix now.

Set the Tone for Others

When you share the concept of deliberate practice and model the behaviors, others will adopt them, too. Among the life-long benefits we can give our students is the motivation to work hard, the capacity overcome obstacles, and skills to persevere. We will do that by leading and modeling deliberate practice.

Those who set out to deliberately improve their leadership skills know they must repeatedly engage in overcoming the challenges, tasks, and activities that are most difficult.

Lesson 11

Effective Classroom Management

Classroom management and discipline are often misconstrued. Discipline is an important part of managing students in any learning environment. Discipline originates from the word *disciple*, which means to follow prescribed teachings. Management deals more with organizational structures. For children and youth to attain the qualities of good discipline (whatever that might mean to you), they must be taught. Effective classroom management involves both teaching and supervising (continuous checking for understanding). Daily organizational routines focused on guidelines that teach good behavior greatly reduce most management issues and challenges. Classroom management strategies combined with teaching and clearly defined structures help create a positive learning environment. What follows are some time-honored strategies.

Know Your Students

Talk with them. Ask questions. Help them dream and learn communication skills and work habits that lead to positive accomplishment. You can't create a family or team concept in an afterschool program without allowing students to freely express themselves, help them get know each other, and permit them to openly interact with the staff. Establish time, routines, and activities that support appropriate sharing and bonding.

Encourage Participants to Help Develop Guidelines

The older students become, the more they understand what is expected from their own behavior as well as others. Most want to learn in a positive environment. They dislike the tension that a lack of structure creates. So, allow them to describe for each other what good behaviors should look, sound, and feel like, especially regarding their respect for self, others, property, and the learning environment.

Establish Consistent Routines

Program staff must work together from a set of common knowledge and expectations for managing students. Students will respond well in most settings if they are provided with clear directions and are consistently taught appropriate behaviors for listening, speaking, interacting, transitioning, respecting personal space – alone and in teams. It is the responsibility of the afterschool program site director to teach the details and expectations of management and supervision expectations to the staff, who in turn teach the students.

Set the Tone, Creatively

Creating a learning environment that is different from school, yet complementary to it, is challenging, especially when the program is housed in a school. Effective planning is essential, especially with the school's principal. There are many creative ways to structure learning environments, yet none attain effectiveness without the leader's vision and commitment to developing a positive workplace. A leader's positive attitude is essential.

Provide an Engaging Curriculum

Boredom is an indicator of ineffective management. You'd eventually act out if you were placed in a work climate with purposeless routines and lack of expectations. Everyone does better when they feel involved, respected, share a sense of belonging, have a voice, and recognize relevant challenges that have a clear purpose and meaning in their lives. Children and youth respond appropriately when they are properly engaged.

Celebrate Diversity

Conflicts may occur when teachers and students come from different cultural backgrounds. Definitions and expectations of appropriate discipline, behavior, and supervision are culturally influenced. Encourage open discussions of culturally responsive classroom management strategies.

Recognize and celebrate students' cultural backgrounds. Commit to building a caring learning environment. Identify common understandings and goals. Calmly respond to adversity with a reinforcement of routines, structures, and expectations that are essential in a middle-class learning environment – after school.

> **It is the responsibility of the afterschool program site-director to teach the details and expectations of management and supervision expectations to the staff, who in turn teach the students.**
>
> **Paul G. Young, Ph.D.**

Coping with Work Refusals

For a variety of reasons, kids sometimes just refuse to start assigned tasks. The refusal may be because of a headache, boredom, anger, or other social-emotional challenges of which you might not be aware. Whatever the reason, kids who refuse to work are in their own way reaching out for help, and as a professional – front line staff as well as program leaders – you must help them. Focus on solutions and assistance rather than punitive consequences.

Here are some recommended do's and don'ts to share with frontline staff for kids who refuse to do assigned work:

DON'T:

- **Become negative.** Punishment usually pushes kids further away, especially when they view it as harsh, mean, and uncaring. Children reacting to trauma do not need more negativity in their lives. Many adults feel it is improper to "let the child get away with" a refusal of reasonable directions or commands. However, using logic, instead of allowing emotions to take over, leads to better outcomes.
- **Remove students.** A familiar consequence for misbehavior is to send a child to the hallway or remove them from the room. Unfortunately, it's not a good solution and often makes things worse. When a staff member's repertoire of re-directive strategies is limited to sending a child the program administrator's office, they've given up authority to manage. Kids know those adults are weak and will push their buttons. Routine student management problems should be dealt with by the professional closest to the situation.
- **Engage in power struggles.** Too much energy gets wasted and no one ever wins. In the end, everyone becomes resentful.
- **Don't make threats**. As a staff, plan strategies for dealing with refusals before confronting them. What you say and do should remain professional and consequences should fit the offense.
- **Don't embarrass**. Take your time, remain calm, and when possible, deal with the student away from others.

DO:

- **Keep teaching.** Your program's goal should be to teach all students. So, when adults confront refusals they should continue teaching, talking, and even involving the noncompliant student if they want to participate.

- **Give the child time.** Often, a little wait time is all that is needed. Planned ignoring can be an effective intervention, especially for small behaviors such as crumpling paper, breaking pencils, refusal to open a book. Remember, refusal is most often an attention-seeking behavior.

- **Reflect on adult behavior.** Does the tone of voice or some other mannerism trigger the refusal?

- **Focus on relationship building.** Relationships are everything. Find time to talk with challenging students privately somewhere within the program time in a non-threatening way. All staff members should get to know all your program participants. Once relationships and formed, most students will work because they know the teacher(s) and other program staff care about them.

- **Know the students' ability.** Sometimes, refusals occur because students think the work is just too hard for them. Make adjustments and accommodations if they need interventions with reading, writing, or math. Give them choices. Plan appropriate forms of assistance for each child's unique needs.

- **Utilize incentive plans.** Some work, some don't. Students are motivated by different things. Find out what students would like to work for and draw up appropriate contracts that detail both student and adult responsibilities and what rewards students will earn for completing work.

- **Plan.** Proactively preparing for incidents of refusal is better than reacting without clarity of how to respond. Develop signals to quietly summon assistance if situations escalate beyond what one adult can handle. Teach positive behaviors and de-escalation strategies – both for students and adults.

- **Work with parents and regular school officials.** Find out if anything at home might be a reason for non-compliance during school and afterschool hours. Develop positive relationships with parents. Complaining that a child is lazy or refuses to work is not an effective strategy for collaboration. Proactive approaches are always better. Share the responsibility for solving problems as well as achieving success.

Adopt this statement as your program mantra.

"Do what you say you will do when you say you will do it."

Paul G. Young, Ph.D.

Lesson 12

Increasing Parent Involvement

Parent involvement has an enormous impact on schools and afterschool programs. Research shows that it has a positive correlation on academic achievement. Where it is lacking, it is considered one of the biggest problems facing schools and afterschool programs. Yet despite what research identifies and predicts, many afterschool program leaders continue to struggle with the issue. Program leaders in affluent communities deal with issues presented by highly visible, proactive parents while those in poorer neighborhoods struggle to effectively engage more than a handful. Despite all that is known, increasing parent involvement can be a very daunting task upon an already full plate.

Create a Vision of Parent Involvement

The first step toward increasing parent involvement is to clearly envision what can be managed if all parents *were* involved. Can your staff deal with the added responsibility? Are they properly trained to build relationships with hard-to-connect-with adults? Can they convey a perception that they really want parents to be involved? How should you measure parent involvement? Is it the number of parents that attend family night events or the quality of the involvement of participants? Are the activities of parent involvement in afterschool aligned with those of the regular school day? Envisioning realities to these questions and determining a baseline are the first steps toward improving parent involvement.

Focus on Varied Types of Parent Involvement

Volunteering is the most common and visible type of parent involvement. But volunteering can be challenging for working parents. Focus on additional activities such as teaching practical parenting and communication skills, learning strategies for the home, conflict management, and decision making. Great strides toward increasing parent engagement will be realized when meaningful communication between the afterschool program and parents occurs regularly and is initiated both ways. It must be open, genuine, respectful, and in a style and language that is comfortable and understood. One-to-one conferences should be held during a student's enrollment and no less than once other times throughout the year. Everyone will appreciate relevant, practical assistance with parenting skills and peer support dealing with common issues of rearing families. Often, a one-to-one approach is most effective and increases involvement.

Communication is Key

It is more beneficial to develop regular forms of two-way communication with parents than to increase attendance at sit-and-get family night activities. Those events have a purpose. But they must also be relevant and meaningful to parents and be a part of regular communication initiatives via newsletters, email, phone, video, and face-to-face.

Teach Everyone

Invite parents for specific lessons and demonstrations. The insights they will develop from observing staff interact with their children will be invaluable. Afterschool program leaders must accept the responsibility of teaching the whole child, and that includes the child's parents, siblings, grandparents, neighbors, and anyone who influences the child. Don't allow poor student management or time-on-task issues to interfere with opportune times to teach everyone that is important to the child's development.

Encourage Parent Advocacy

Parents can be the best advocates for your afterschool program. Where their presence is valued, and social interactions commonly occur with the staff and among other parents, they will be the most effective at recruiting shy parents to become more involved. Trained effectively, they can raise resources, arrange trips, and provide stimulating experiences that create a welcoming, family environment. The program director sets the tone by smiling and extending the first handshake.

The National PTA has developed the National Standards for Family-School Partnerships Implementation Guide, a tool for empowering people to work together with an end goal of building family-school partnerships and student success. Those standards provide a framework for six types of involvement:

1 – Welcoming All Families
2 – Communicating Effectively
3 – Supporting Student Success
4 – Speaking Up for Every Child
5 – Sharing Power
6 – Collaborating with the Community

https://www.pta.org/home/run-your-pta/National-Standards-for-Family-School-Partnerships

Lesson 13

Tips for Improving Public Speaking

For some people, just the thought of speaking in public can lead to debilitation. But for others, anticipation of a public speaking event elevates the nerves and creates a sense of stage fright that most learn to manage. While there are those that never become comfortable in the public eye, others gain confidence and learn strategies that help them manage stage fright, deliver the goods, and reap the benefits of an effective performance. What follows are pieces of advice and tips designed to help afterschool professionals avoid embarrassment and improve their public speaking opportunities.

Stage Fright Is Normal

Even the most veteran and respected celebrities suffer from varying degrees of stage fright. Most will admit that a heightened state of nervousness pushes them to prepare, concentrate and do a better job than when relaxed. Like learning to swim, you first must get in the water. Don't shy away from opportunities to share what you do, talk about your program, and tell the afterschool story. Public speaking ranges from standing on stage in front of thousands to speaking with community groups or even your governing board. Do your homework. Know your facts. The more you speak publicly, the easier it gets.

Develop a Postive Presence

Before you speak, look in the mirror and assure that you look like a professional. Present yourself with a friendly face and a natural smile. Make eye contact with your audience. Take a deep breath, stand or sit up straight, adjust your notes and microphone (use it if and when it is available), thank the person who introduced you and say something nice about him or her. Recognizing and perfecting this simple sequence of events can help you catch your breath and settle into a speaking mode.

Use Correct Grammar and Diction

Nothing is more embarrassing for a "professional" than to speak with incorrect grammar. It's simply unacceptable. Likewise, practice softening the effects regional dialects and perfect the pronunciation of challenging words. Speak with a tempo that is easily understood. Musicians understand how to include nuances, dynamics, and inflections that add interest to the music and the spoken word. Seek out their advice and mentorship when practicing for a public event.

Connect with the Audience

Your listeners are present to see and hear you. You are providing them with new thoughts or information about accepted practices. They recognize you as the expert and want to hear your story. Prepare in advance by learning about the demographics and experiences of those you will address and gear your remarks toward them. Arrive early, check out the venue, test the acoustics, and interact with those already present. This will help you warm up to the room and enable your listeners to begin connecting with you.

Stories are Powerful

People expect PowerPoint presentations filled with charts, diagrams, pictures, and data analysis, and without doubt, those are important ingredients of presentations. But listeners will better relate with you through the powerful stories that you tell because it is a natural part of language. Stories help connect because they contain emotion. They provide intuitive insights and help you persuade listeners to accept your way of thinking. Undoubtedly, when done well, telling your story will help you transfer your ideas to others in effective ways. Practice telling your personal story. It creates your brand.

Visualize Your Performance

An adage suggests that practice makes perfect. We may never achieve perfection, but we can improve each time we speak. The key is to develop a heightened sense of awareness of how you look, act, and sound. Videotape yourself. Analyze what you see and hear afterwards. Reflect and assess the comfort level, smile, eye contact, humor, and the timbre and tempo of your voice. Imagine yourself giving a speech worthy of a standing ovation. Thinking positively leads to success. Bravo!

When you speak in public, you perform like an actor on a stage.
Perception is important. Dress appropriately.
Present a professional image to your audience.
Look pleasant, enthusiastic, confident, and proud. Remain calm.
Appear relaxed, even if you feel nervous. Speak slowly, enunciate clearly, and show appropriate emotion and feeling relating to your topic.

"LIKE, ELIMINATE 'UMS' AND 'AHS', RIGHT?"

"LIKE," "UM," "AH," AND "YOU KNOW"
ARE
PROFESSIONAL CREDIBILITY KILLERS

You will sound better than others when you avoid using
"ummm"
to begin your thoughts.

Which is better?

Tell us your name and what you do.

#1. *Ummm*, my name is Annie AfterSchool, *ummm,* and, *like*, I'm the director of, *ummm*, Main Street AfterSchool Program.

#2. My name is Annie AfterSchool, and I'm the director of Main Street AfterSchool Program.

Lesson 14

Listen to How You Sound

Does your voice reflect your personality? Better yet, when you speak, do you sound like a confident leader? Are you able to adjust and adapt the sound of your voice to fit various situations and match your message? If you are like most people, you probably don't enjoy hearing a recording of your voice. And maybe you've never thought much about how your voice reflects your personality, but it does. An understanding of vocal skills is important for all leaders. Practice is essential. We all can improve.

Rate of Speech

Most people can speak between 120 and 150 words a minute. Get a recorder, select something that you can comfortably read aloud, and time yourself. You will likely fall somewhere within that continuum. You don't want to speak so fast or with such force that people can't understand you, but you also don't want to be a bore. Speed projects charisma; slowness projects laziness. Slowness can be frustrating for the listener. It is better to speak a bit faster than it is to be slower paced.

Volume of Speech

Musicians are trained to utilize the appeal of dynamic contrasts. Music that is excessively loud or soft is boring. Similar to the rate of speech, it is better to be a little louder than soft because you can be heard more easily. Everyone can recall at least one experience of enduring a monotone speaker. Contrasts are essential. Use them. When you do speak softly, it forces people to listen more closely. Don't shout. To create interest, focus on using a variety of dynamic levels.

Diction and Grammar

Don't slur, mispronounce, or add extra syllables to words. Say "you" instead of "ya" and "going to" rather than "gonna." One could easily add other examples. As for grammar, there is no place - nor any excuse - for grammatical errors by afterschool leaders. But the mistakes we've heard growing up are hard to shake. Listen and observe others. If you know you have room for improvement, ask your mentor or trusted friend to point out your diction and grammatical errors and teach you better skills.

Pitch

People will judge you by the tone of your voice. Speak too high and you will sound immature; too low and you might be accused of being overly serious. Learn how to use contrasts and shape sentences so that there are high and low points.

Rhythm

Know your situation. We utilize different rhythms in our voices on the playground than we do the library. Adjust. Don't be a monotone.

Timber

You don't want to sound nasal, throaty, breathy, tentative, or hoarse. The cheerleader or football coach voice is not likely to sound appropriate in the afterschool program. Timbre (pronounced as TAM-bər with a soft a) is the character or quality of a musical sound or voice as distinct from its pitch and intensity. Timber enables listeners to distinguish different qualities of sound. A harshness of timber when correcting students may be perceived negatively and become a huge block in relationship building.

Avoid Non-Words (Verbal Graffiti)

Avoid using "uh," "ah," "um," "you know," "well," or many other "filler" sounds or words. They are known as verbal graffiti. And above all, use the word "like" only when it would be appropriately used. (Don't forget to read and re-read Lesson 13 about the dangers of verbal graffiti).

Regional and Ethnic Accents

We all possess regional and ethnic accents. Most add appeal and unique qualities to our speech. But if your accent causes you to be misunderstood, it is likely too heavy. Learn to tone it down.

Tips for Giving a Great Speech
(or Talking on the Phone)

- Posture – Sit and/or stand with correct posture. If you don't, you'll impact your air supply and others will hear the difference.
- Breath normally – Take deep breaths at normal times. When speaking, if you become short of breath, something else is wrong.
- Open your mouth — You can't pronounce words with closed lips.
- Eye contact – Look at people and project your voice. Don't move your hands, shuffle papers, or sneak glances at your email's inbox.
- KISS – Keep it short and simple. Use shorter sentences with pauses so that your listeners can catch up with you. Smile and add humor.

Paul G. Young, Ph.D.

Lesson 15

Help Students (and Adults) Become Better Listeners

At some time, every afterschool leader questions whether anyone really listens to them, whether it be students or adults. When you give basic announcements, you observe kids (or adults) talking, playing with gadgets, fidgeting, or staring away. Increasingly, kids ask adults to repeat directions seconds after they have been told what to do. People complain yet approach basic and routine communications in much the same way every day. We can do better. We can improve.

Insist on Quiet and Attention

To produce the best results, structure the time, place, and environment where group instructions are made. Get down to the level of your listeners. It adds comfort. From the outset, provide explicit lessons on the importance of listening to help students (or adults) improve their skills. Teach basic listening expectations and the importance of respect for others who are talking. When outside, gather the group closely around you. Indoors, provide a place for listeners to sit instead of standing. Reduce distracting environmental noises. Before speaking, make sure everyone has stopped talking and is making eye contact with the speaker.

Provide Verbal and Written Communications

Many daily informational and instructional directions are routine. Write them down. Then, while speaking to the group, direct their attention to your written work. This not only reduces the number of repetitive questions, but it's far easier to point to written directions than respond to those inevitable repeated questions, "What are we supposed to do?"

Connect with the Eyes and the Ears

Eye contact between listeners and speakers is essential. Scan your audience before you begin to speak. Don't start unless listeners' eyes are focused in your direction and there is quiet within the room. Listen while you are speaking and stop and wait for students to redirect if their attention drifts away. Use your eyes to assess for listeners' understanding. Use your ears to show how you want others to listen to you when they are speaking.

Limit Directions to Three

Don't assume people will be able to remember a long list of everything you say. Limit your information, directions, or requests to no more than three. More than that, listeners become confused.

Ask for a Paraphrased Response

For your most challenged or selective listeners, insist that they respond by paraphrasing what has been said in a complete sentence. This works to help them focus. They will listen more intently knowing they must reply and that they must use words correctly that have been included in the directions.

Accommodate for Disorders

Some kids have processing disorders. Pairing them with others for a repeat of instructions, with an adult listening in for accuracy, saves time and builds a sense of community. There may always be some students or adults who display listening "challenges" no matter what you do. For some, they are just seeking your attention. For those differently-abled, work to enable them to succeed in the mainstream.

Be a Role Model

A loud and angry voice is frightening, and when people are nervous or scared, it is more difficult for them to listen. Avoid sarcasm. Be calm. At all times, you must use correct grammar. Use dynamic contrasts in your vocal tone to create interest and stress important points. When you finish speaking, model the listening behaviors that you want others to show you. Listening skills take time to develop and require patience and consistency to teach. They are among the most challenging skills for young learners to develop, and yet also one of the most important. By developing an ability to listen well, we increase the ability to understand, use vocabulary, and attain independence.

 Listening skills are an invaluable part of life. Children, youth, and adults with good listening skills perform better, enjoy more success in social relationships, and have a better frustration tolerance.

Paul G. Young, Ph.D.

Lesson 16

Dealing with Difficult Staff

Most people working in afterschool programs are dedicated, hard-working individuals who have committed themselves to the welfare and care of children and youth. Yet, if we are honest with ourselves, we also work with some who, at best, are difficult to get along with. An outstanding staff is the key to quality and success. Because of the work they do, it is imperative that every afterschool professional have a positive and proactive manner working with children. Yet, some choose not to behave that way. These individuals test the resolve of every afterschool leader.

Characteristics of Difficult Staff Members

Difficult staff members are negative, stubborn, argumentative, rude, lazy, domineering, cynical, resistant to change, inflexible, and sometimes just plain boring. On top of those issues, they just aren't good with kids. Their negativity and ineffectiveness weighs anchor on others. You would do whatever it takes to make sure that your own child was never assigned to any class or activity with them.

Focus on Clarifying Basic Expectations

To be motivated, all staff members need to know what is expected of them. Provide written memos that explain what work is to be done, clarify your beliefs and values, and focus efforts toward essential goals.

Praise Authentically

Everyone responds to praise. With difficult staff, make sure what is said is consistent and honest. Public praise can and should be used if it isn't resented by the positive staff. But don't continue to praise mediocres in public if improvements aren't made. And be careful what you write. Inauthentic or forced attempts to "catch them being good" might later haunt you during formal reviews.

Raise Discomfort Levels

If you never turn up the heat, nothing will change. Factually tell difficult staff members how they come across to others. Work with them to assume personal responsibility for complaints from others. Get their attention by recognizing and empowering the positive performers.

Weaken Opportunities for Difficult Influences

Divide and conquer. Assign seats during meetings so that you have proximity to negative staff. They will complain less when nearest you. Structure agendas and expectations so it is clear who speaks, when, where, and how. Communicate your expectations for informal conversation and explain your tolerance levels for gossip and griping. Teach all staff to brainstorm and suggest potential solutions to problems when they identify them.

Understand the Dynamics of Negative Leadership

There is a wise farmer's saying that suggests that you "Never wrestle with a pig. You both get dirty and the pig loves it." Another is "Never argue with an idiot. People watching may not be able to tell the difference." Rather than allowing yourself to instinctively "take on" difficult staff, take away their audience. Never try to win an argument in public. And as hard as it may be to do so, allow opportunities for your challengers to save face.

Reseat Your Staff on Your Bus

Break up groups by reassigning duties, restructuring work stations, and reconfiguring other external factors where negativity develops. Place people in strategic leadership roles to attain buy-in. Clarify your vision and teach expectations. Once you are confident that everyone understands, move forward.

Know When to Cut Your Losses

Many difficult workers will leave when the heat gets turned up. But for a few, nothing works. You will validate inappropriate behavior if you ignore their ineffective performance. You must implement a formal dismissal using due process with factual and objective documentation. These experiences are usually stressful, but stay focused on what is best for the kids and the program. If you act like a professional, you are unlikely to achieve negative results. You are more likely to have far-reaching positive influence on the rest of your staff.

"Never wrestle with a pig. You both get dirty, and the pig loves it."

"Never argue with an idiot. People watching may not be able to tell the difference."

69

Typical Distribution of Adult Performance

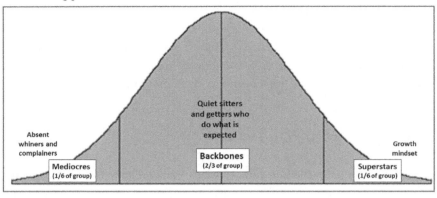

There are three types workers among any typical staff. The largest group are the Backbones (2/3) who regularly come to work, do what is expected, do what is best for kids, and make your program work. The other third is typically divided between mediocres and superstars. Then leader's goal is to move the entire staff in the direction of the superstars to follow their example. When the mediocres are allowed to dominate, the program culture suffers.

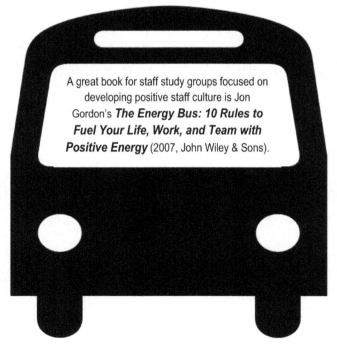

A great book for staff study groups focused on developing positive staff culture is Jon Gordon's *The Energy Bus: 10 Rules to Fuel Your Life, Work, and Team with Positive Energy* (2007, John Wiley & Sons).

Lesson 17

Reframing Issues

Like it or not, there are times when practices inevitably change and we must creatively find ways to lead and do our work differently. One of those practices involves budgeting. As most state and local governments adopt smaller operating budgets, spending practices change. Afterschool leaders must refocus our issues and develop common talking points that become part of the more-with-less plan, not a perpetuation of the budget crisis. We must adjust our advocacy efforts and communicate with government leaders in ways that help them view afterschool as a creative, determined, and reliable strategy for addressing multiple issues facing children, youth, and families.

Reframe Afterschool as a Proactive Issue

The pendulum of change moved in a conservative direction following the 2010 midterm elections. Elected politicians of both parties were challenged to trim the size of government, reduce taxes, control spending, and balance budgets. Voters desperately called for meaningful, secure jobs and a brighter future. Any issues that we have in afterschool that appear to add to the spending crisis will not be heard. Therefore, we need to reframe afterschool as a strategy to be included in solutions that create better jobs for families and a sustainable workforce.

Develop Relationships

Elected leaders want to do good for their constituents. They know that building relationships is key to their tenure and success. They need relationships with us, and likewise, we need them on our side. We have a critical opportunity to shape and proactively position afterschool as a nonpartisan issue and an important component of local community plans that address societal concerns and reinvigorate the family and workforce opportunities.

Create News

Perhaps now more than ever, we must clearly demonstrate the benefits of afterschool. An important way to do that is by telling stories. We all have a repertoire of important, attention-grabbing stories and testimonials. The key is that we must engage the media to help us communicate our issues and stories. Interpersonal relationships are essential. Testimonials from upbeat reporters/storytellers are hard for anyone to ignore.

Unite Around Common Talking Points

Everyone is looking for ways to create a positive, secure, sustainable future. The public and investors will support initiatives that are accountable and yield results. Collectively, our voices will be heard when we focus on:

- Economic Development. Working families must have safe and nurturing afterschool programs to be productive at work.
- Workforce Development. Time in afterschool programs helps children and youth learn valuable academic, physical, technical, social, emotional, and creative skills that will prepare them for jobs that haven't yet been invented.
- Scientific Development. Our country's position as a world leader will be jeopardized if we fail to motivate, teach, and inspire children and youth to understand, appreciate, and engage in scientific careers. We must embrace STEM and STEAM learning initiatives afterschool and clearly demonstrate how they help students prepare for their future and ours.
- Community Development. Afterschool programs provide opportunities for community service, mentoring, collaborative networking, and business partnerships that strengthen connections within communities. A cohesive community that values and expects rigorous academic, fitness, and nutrition standards for all children and youth will view afterschool as an integral part of attaining those ideals.

There is non-partisan support for afterschool. But in this era, we must show data and proof of success. We must renew and reframe efforts to show that afterschool investments are essential for our future.

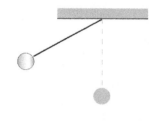

As the political agenda pendulum swings between liberal and conservative camps, we must adjust our advocacy efforts and communicate with new leaders in ways that help them view afterschool as a creative solution strategy for addressing common issues facing children and families.

Paul G. Young, Ph.D.

Lesson 18

What, How, and Why

Over time, assumptions develop that paralyze thinking, slow growth, and stymie progress in any profession. Assumptions influence how afterschool professionals respond to what they do and how they do it. Because of that, when asked the more important question of WHY an afterschool programs exists, many people stumble and mumble a response. Those who lead best clearly understand their organization's mission and can succinctly explain WHY they (and the  organization) do WHAT they do and HOW they do it. But all too often, we are first asked WHAT we do? We need to learn to reorder the questions, starting with WHY.

Why?

Again, if someone were to ask what happens in an afterschool program, most leaders can provide an adequate answer complete with examples. They describe program objectives, goals, outcomes, services, and job functions. Those are easy to identify. But when asked why an afterschool program exists, few leaders have practiced articulating a response. The WHY is the organization's mission, its purpose, and its core values. Why should someone care that an afterschool program exists? The better we can answer the WHY question, the better we can address the hows and whats. Inspirational leaders never lose focus of the WHY. Whys are beliefs. Hows are actions that realize those beliefs. Whats are the results of actions. An articulate WHY response always challenges the status quo.

How?

Most afterschool leaders know HOW they do what they do. HOW responses describe the ways that services are provided and imply good processes, strategies, and standards of performance. The assumption is that the HOW sets the program apart, differentiating it from others with compelling evidence of effectiveness. Staff members within an afterschool program are often motivated to do the hows because of a series of carrots and sticks. Yet, the hows don't inspire loyalty or trust in a program any better than the whats. When everyone clearly understands and buys into the core mission of WHY and afterschool program exists, the hows and the whats better begin to make sense.

What?

WHAT an afterschool program does is the result of its HOW actions – how it creates services, develops a culture, and benefits for children, youth, and adults. People will know what a leader believes (and what afterschool programs accomplish) by observing the things that they say and do over time. Afterschool program leaders who can clearly articulate why they do their work and how they do it will sound authentic to their followers. These days, most everyone can differentiate when answers to questions are nothing more than politically correct. Inspirational afterschool leaders cannot be politically correct and always be authentic. Leaders are authentic when everything they say and do is firmly based on what they believe. Authenticity matters.

Reorder the Questions

Great afterschool programs have a great WHY. Those programs acquire loyal patrons, partners, and stakeholders when their leaders stay focused on the WHY. It requires a clear vision to lead a great afterschool program. Leaders do not inspire when they chase new fads and veer from a steady course. Instead, they confuse. Energy and charisma are important, but clarity and authenticity are essential. Effective afterschool program leaders never waver from their WHY. They continuously challenge assumptions. They create programs where people want to work, and loyalty is high.

When the WHY is clear, grant-funded programs succeed and their leader will find ways to make them sustainable. When the why, how, and what questions are conceived in the right order and properly balanced, people will want to work in afterschool programs, trust-levels will be high among all stakeholders, and positive outcomes will be prevalent. Because all staff members have influence, when they each understand and are taught how to articulate the relationships between the why, hows, and whats of the program, the final whats that emerge will make the program remarkable. When people really believe in what they do, and can explain WHY, everything they say will be authentic and believable.

People do not care so much about what afterschool programs do.

They are inspired much more about

WHY

they do what they do and how they do it.

Lesson 19

Learn to Ask Why Five Times

When solving problems, especially trying to find the root cause, afterschool program directors often ask "why?" When working with kids, and even adults, their typical response is often "because." If you fail to delve deeper, "because" results in little understanding. By using a more persistent approach, starting with the result and working backwards and continually asking "why" at least five times, the root cause of the problem becomes more apparent. This approach is called the 5-Whys Technique[2], a simple tool that is easy to learn and apply with many common problems.

Ask the First Why

By asking "why" five times, one can usually peel away the layers of symptoms that hide the cause of a problem. Suppose your problem is that your staff and volunteers are complaining about your school-based program participants being loud and disrespectful as they enter your afterschool program. Gathering your team and clarifying the problem, you ask the first why. (1) "Why are our participants loud and disrespectful when our program begins?" Answers might vary, but if you hear this one, "They don't know how to behave," you reply by asking, (2) "Why don't our participants know how to behave?"

The Second Why

It is at this point where errors often occur. Don't jump to conclusions, assign blame, or react to answers you can't control. Teach people what you are trying to do with the 5-whys. Listen, then ask the next why. Your response might be "Why is that?" Or try, (2) "Why don't our participants

² From the Toyota Production System in the 1970s

79

know how to behave?" Again, responses will vary, but you might hear "because they've been sitting in school all day!" Listen, then respond by framing the third why. (3) "Why does sitting all day cause them to misbehave?"

The Third Why

Probe deeper by continuously searching for systemic causes of the problem. Again, you might simply ask "why is that?", or frame the third why as (3) "Why does sitting all day cause our participants to misbehave?" Among varied answers, you might hear (4) "They don't have any recess time."

The Fourth Why

As you listen to, "They don't have any recess time," you could simply ask "why is that? Or better, you can guide the probe with (4) "Why does not having recess time cause our students to be loud and disrespectful?" As this point, the root cause should become clearer. If not, continue to ask why. Among varied responses you might hear (5) "They don't have time to release energy." Or "They don't know who to handle themselves when structure is loose." Or "They've not been taught how to behave."

The Fifth Why

It is at this point that a root cause to the problem will likely emerge. As you ask your fifth why, (5) "why is that?" the answers will likely become obvious. In this scenario, the root cause could be (a) a disconnect of expectations between school and afterschool, (b) a developmental issue caused by lack of play time, (c) poor supervision, (d) a lack of teaching of expectations, or more.

The Benefits and Shortcomings of the Five Whys

The 5-whys technique is a simple problem-solving tool. It tempers emotions and keeps the team focused on the problem and the solution. After a little practice, it is easy to implement, especially for problems that are related to human interactions. However, if you recognize that a problem is more complex, the technique is not likely to lead to a "right" answer. When that is evident, more sophisticated problem-solving techniques are necessary. Also, with the 5-whys, it is possible that different people will identify different causes to the same problem. The simplicity of the technique is likely its downfall. Yet, most all problem-solving techniques have shortcomings and limits to definitive solutions. The 5-whys provides teams with a high degree of freedom in their thinking process.

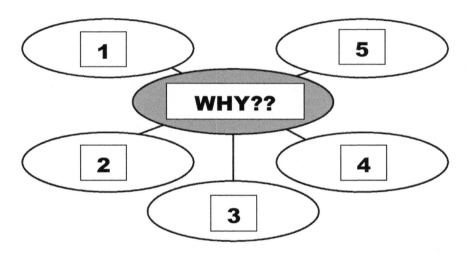

Repeatedly asking "why" five times peels away the layers of symptoms which can lead to the root cause of a problem. The 5-why technique is easy to learn and very effective with young children that are driving you crazy.

Paul G. Young, Ph.D.

Lesson 20

How to Boost Your Resume

From time to time, it is a good practice for afterschool professionals to assess their current work status and be on the lookout for future job opportunities that have growth potential and even better conditions for career advancement. To grow, everyone needs intellectual challenges, and some jobs simply lack adequate stimulation for upwardly mobile professionals. It is a good habit to regularly update professional resumes. Following are some advice tips that can give your resume a boost.

Join Your Professional Association

Many resume readers are long-time, dues-paying members of professional associations. They make connections with potential job candidates with whom they share relevant experiences. Employers will be impressed when they see that a candidate for a program leadership position lists examples of involvement and contributions in your state membership organization. Never fail to list years of consistent membership with NAA and your state affiliate organizations.

Volunteer

Volunteer in your professional associations. Volunteering provides a variety of benefits. You can learn new skills, expand your professional network, and make influential connections. Participate in committees. Accept leaderships roles. Contribute to special projects where you can accentuate your special interests, such as social media management, technology, or entreprenurial skills. Potential employers want employees who are not afraid to share what they know and give back to others.

Highlight Professional Endeavors and Interests

What else might set you apart from the field of candidates? If you speak one or more foreign languages, list that important skill. If you aren't bilingual, list any classes you might have taken that accentuate your global interests. Detail your special tech skills, business experience, other job-related knowledge and competencies needed for the job you are seeking. Take advantage of every opportunity to showcase your well-rounded capacities. Writing, speaking, fitness activities, hobbies, music, and other artist endeavors provide resume richness and depth.

Highlight Technology Skills

Website development, management, and design skills may not seem relevant for people seeking to lead afterschool programs. But when budgets are tight, your experience and ability to utilize and help maintain a program's technology platform, advise, and help other's implement key program strategies might make you stand out most. Learn what potential employers might want and need, then provide details that accentuate special skills you can bring to the job.

Tap Your Network

Through your involvement and volunteer work in your professional membership associations, you can build an extensive specialist network. Tap into that network when seeking jobs. Tailor your resume to meet the unique requirements of different jobs. Standard resumes are not always adequate. Resumes serve the purpose of getting you an interview, not a job. A successful interview will land you the job.

Like it or not, employers will usually make a judgment about your resume in five seconds. Under this timeframe, the most important aspect will be the titles that you listed on the resume, so make sure they grab attention. Try to be as descriptive as possible, giving the employer a good idea about the nature of your past work experiences.

Resumes that include a long list of "responsibilities included…" are routine, but not always efficient in selling yourself. Instead of listing responsibilities, therefore, describe your professional achievements.

Tailor your resume for a specific employer by identifying what possible problems are at hand. Contacts within your professional network can help you understand employer's needs, then adjust your resume to clearly and professionally show how you and your skills would help to solve those problems and create conditions of success.

To grow, everyone needs intellectual challenges, and some jobs simply lack adequate stimulation for upwardly mobile professionals.

It is good practice to regularly update professional resumes.

Lesson 21

Crafting a Ten-Second Commercial

Some people seem to be able to work a room and make instant, spontaneous connections while others are more reserved and tend to keep to themselves. First impressions are important. They set the tone for success and influence how people will respond. What are the secrets of those who can quickly establish rapport, build relationships, and get others to embrace and act on their ideas?

Establish Eye Contact and Smile

You indicate confidence when you look another person in the eye. You signal approachability when you smile. When you do, it's human nature for the other person to smile back. Eyes give direction and focus meaning on the words we say. We also tend to synchronize behaviors with others. If you relax, so will others. Show tension, and others will mimic it. So, calm down, convince yourself to get in a welcoming mood, put on your best smile, observe body language, and listen to the verbal cues of the people you meet.

Know What You Want

There are only a few ways you can get people to do what you want them to do, such as with legal, financial, physical, or emotional force. Persuasion is more efficient. But if you fail making a first impression - which opens the door for persuasion - you must resort to the others. To be convincing, gain trust, and get into others' imagination, you have to know what it is that you want from them and what you want them to do. The key is being creative and able to change until you get what you want.

Choose a Useful Attitude

Attitudes are real, and through them we train the emotions. There are three useful attitudes for making connections. Enthusiasm infects others with excitement, energy, and vitality. Curiosity shows others that you want to know what is going on with them and that you are evolving and growing. Humility demonstrates that you are modest and focused on serving others. Useful attitudes trigger behaviors of vigor and openness.

Practice Your 10-Second Commercial

So, once you've mastered your attitude, body language, and congruently synched them with your voice, you have the potential to convince others to connect with you. But if you talk too fast or too slow, you'll lose people. When you meet someone for the first time, you have about 10 seconds to impress them. To succeed, practice explaining what you do, who you do it for, and how it benefits the listener. Script your commercial. Memorize it. Practice for ease with rhythm and flow. Keep practicing it until people ask to know more. Then, you have about 20 additional seconds to solidify the connection.

Your Commercial is a Mini-Presentation

Your 10-second commercial can be used on the phone, at a professional meeting, a party, or even in an elevator – anywhere you meet people. It is an engaging, artfully crafted presentation intended to impress and hook people into wanting to know more about you. An effective 10-second commercial coveys the value and essence of what you do.

Dress for Success

Your looks matter. Your image has a very real impact on how effectively you can convince people to connect with you, how people can imagine you as a professional colleague, and whether they will support your career advancement. The way you choose to dress should reflect the personality you want to convey in the workplace. Even though you may meet many people virtually, you'll feel better about yourself if you've dressed for success.

Practice Introducing Yourself

Sometimes, you must introduce yourself in daunting environments. Your 10-second commercial will be an invaluable and reliable overture. Then, focus on your attitude and synchronization with the other person. Seek common ground. Smile, listen, speak comfortably, and enjoy the outcomes!

Your 10-second commercial must communicate what you do, who you do it for, and why it is meaningful to other people.
Keep it short and simple.
When you've polished it to the point
that people you offer it to ask to hear more,
you've delivered an effective 10-second commercial.

Paul G. Young, Ph.D.

Lesson 22

Email Communication Cautions

Email has made communication with parents, staff, and colleagues much faster, easier, and less expensive than traditional forms of mail. There are many positive benefits from the conveniences of email. Unfortunately, users can also suffer negative consequences when it is used unprofessionally. For those using computers or  other electronic communication devices that are property of the public schools, email can become an admissible document in legal cases. Afterschool professionals must use caution and avoid the familiarities that have become widespread in the age of texting, tweeting, and more.

Keep Email Communication Professional and Use Proper Etiquette

Not everyone understands the text message abbreviations that cross into email communications. It is best to write with correct spelling and grammar. Accurate and attractive looking email communications are important and make a good impression.

Be Aware of the Tone

The tone of an email message, especially if it is about a serious concern, a question, or a sensitive student issue, must be clear to the recipient. Be aware of how your ideas and thinking might be interpreted. Ask a colleague to read sensitive messages before sending.

Never Write an Email When You Are Angry

Because of the impersonal convenience of email, it is tempting to write about situations or respond to messages in the remoteness of your work space rather than confronting another person who might have angered you. When you write while you are angry, the tone of your message and what you write will likely be harsh, defensive, and possibly make a situation worse. When you reply while angry, your email is accessible forever. Worse, if you mistakenly hit "reply to all," many others will observe your foolishness. On the other hand, putting your thoughts in writing might help you sort out issues from emotion. Write using a program other than email, then copy and paste if necessary when you've calmed down.

Be Responsible and Responsive

Afterschool personnel, like their regular school colleagues, have a responsibility to communicate with parents about their children – and with each other. Email should be acknowledged and responded to within one working day. What you write should be a responsible answer. It is easy to send a quick, informal message to a colleague, but anytime these emails contain reference to a student, the family has a legal right to request copies. It is easy and convenient to write something to a colleague, but caution that it might later be misused or misinterpreted if it becomes forwarded to a parent.

Ethical Issues with Email

Never interfere with others' computer software and files. Only use approved email programs. Do not attempt to sidestep filters and other controls that your place of work has decided are necessary for censorship and protection. Make sure that a discussion about computer ethics is a part of staff orientations and regular training. Always use email in ways that insures consideration and respect for others.

Be Selective of Mailing Lists

Your name on many work-related distribution lists might be required. For many others, it is an option. Be careful what you subscribe to and understand how to unsubscribe if you no longer feel an email distribution list is appropriate or serves a need. Clean your own mailing lists of individuals no longer employed by your agency or connected to your program.

Privacy Rights

Our freedoms and emergent technologies will generate continuous ethical issues for email usage in afterschool. Your school or agency should develop a privacy policy that can be used to help leaders decide what is appropriate usage and what is abuse. Privacy policies will help you determine and teach others what they have a right to do versus what is right to do.

For those using computers or other electronic communication devices that are property of the public schools, email can become an admissible document in legal cases.

Suggested Email Tagline

PLEASE NOTE: This message and any response to it may constitute a public record, and therefore may be available upon request in accordance with [state] public records law.

This e-mail message, including any attachments, is for the sole use of the intended recipient(s) and may contain private, confidential, and/or privileged information. Any unauthorized review, use, disclosure, or distribution is prohibited. If you are not the intended recipient, employee, or agent responsible for delivering this message, please contact the sender by reply e-mail and destroy all copies of the original e-mail message.

Lesson 23

Create Good Impressions with Email and Voice Mail Etiquette

Email has become the preferred method of communication for afterschool professionals. It's easy, inexpensive, and enables instantaneous connections. As the costs of regular mail services increase, email will certainly expand as the preferred method for conducting business. Likewise, texting is commonplace. And most everyone can relate to communicating by voicemail at home, work, and with cellular phones. We commonly use these tools to connect and build relationships. But a surefire way to ruin first impressions and weaken your program's connections, relationships, and reputation, is to display poor voicemail, email, or texting etiquette. To increase professionalism within an organization and to gain an edge working with stakeholders, afterschool leaders should insist their employees understand how, when, where, and why to use electronic communications - and when to avoid them.

Use Proper Spelling, Grammar & Punctuation

Errors give a bad impression and can convey a wrong message. Emails with no full stops or commas are difficult to read and can sometimes even change the meaning of the text. Reread your message before sending and try to "see it" in the eyes of the recipient. Utilize spell checking options and proofread, proofread, proofread.

Create Positives with Voice Messaging

Express positive emotions when creating your personal voicemail message. Have others critique the tone, timbre, and tempo of your voice. Likewise, always strive to leave messages that sound positive, upbeat, and express gratitude. Never allow anger, disappointment, frustration, or sarcasm to influence voicemail messages. You create a personal brand through all forms of communication. Making a poor decision while leaving a voicemail can become a mistake that can haunt you forever.

Develop Concise and Punctual Email Habits

Email is fast. People expect a quick response. Strive to reply within the same working day and take no longer than 24 hours. People will read for only a few seconds, so say what you need to say using the fewest words. If your response must be lengthy and complicated and require time to complete, send a response acknowledging receipt of the original message and explain when you will get back with details. Then follow through responsibly.

Provide Complete Contact Information

Email should start with a personal salutation and end with your complete contact information including phone and mailing address. Auto-replies are usually ineffective. Slow down when leaving voice messages and allow the person you called adequate time to record your return phone number.

Be Polite

Use CAPITAL LETTERS in email to shout! Use them sparingly! Likewise, avoid excessive use of priority features. High-priority messaging usually appears to be more aggressive than need be. Don't use acronyms unless you are sure the recipient is familiar with them. Requesting receipt of delivery will likely annoy most recipients.

Show Respect and Pay Attention

Actively listen to speakers during meetings and presentations. It is disrespectful to read or reply to messages in those settings. Turn off and put away your devices to avoid the temptation.

Nothing Beats Personal Communication

There are times when using electronic communications can be counter-productive. You will build better rapport and enhance relationships with good old-fashioned face-to-face communication. People are more likely to better receive critiques and negative messages in person rather than by email. When in doubt, get away from the computer. Despite the conveniences of computers and cellular phones and the brilliance you might display with them, the most effective way to communicate with human beings is face-to-face in real time.

Connecting with others helps build emotional bonds that enable them to solve problems and feel appreciated, valued, and important.

Relationships are strengthened through communication in real time. Etiquette affects afterschool leaders' efforts to connect and communicate.

Lesson 24

Planning for Leadership Transitions

Leadership is essential for developing and sustaining high quality afterschool programs. The leader sets the tone for the program operations and culture. But everyone at some time will and can be replaced. Although a leadership transition might be exciting and energizing, it can often prove difficult both for the exiting leader, who has a new role, and for the program staff who experience changes in their environment. For them, a leadership transition can be scary because of the unknowns that suddenly begin emerging. An effective transition plan describes the dimensions leadership, charts a process, and explores ways for an organization to groom future leaders. Ultimately, success occurs when two individuals commit to sharing responsibilities for success.

Communicate Intentions Early

It takes time to interview, hire, and train an afterschool program director. Exiting leaders should give their organizations adequate time to find their replacements. No one wants to be a lame duck leader; likewise, no one likes to get blindsided by a sudden leadership change.

Reflect on Program Goals During Searches

The arrival of a new leader provides an opportunity for looking at issues from a different perspective. How might priorities change? Are their opportunities for reorganization? Exiting leaders may have little input into determining their successors, but they can and should describe the needed knowledge, skills, and information that will help others select the most qualified and capable replacement.

Plan Time to Work Together

Even if the new leader comes from within the organization, it takes time to assess, plan, organize, budget, and implement a smooth transition. Both leaders should have time to build new relationships, identify obstacles to change, and work side-by-side. The exiting leader should remain available to consult for a predetermined period of time. A new leader who is not provided opportunties to learn about and focus on the organization's goals is deprived critical time to build trust with their new followers, reshape the program vision, define new expectations, and implement them successfully.

Support Each Other

Assuming any new leadership role can be overwhelming. There are new challenges, demands, administrative tasks, rituals, and systems to learn and individual needs of followers to identify and nurture. New leaders need time to develop networks of mentors and peers who can provide advice and counsel. Likewise, exiting leaders must deal with new opportunities and responsibilities, and sometimes grieve at leaving their beloved program. Either way, it is essential to work closely together, mutually address the dangers and challenges, earn and show respect, and support each other. Never publicly criticize your predecessor.

Organize the Office

Exiting leaders should clean their workspace and update and make accessible all personnel and computer files. Successors will appreciate current contact lists and detailed, clearly marked organizational records.

Plan Ceremonies and Rituals

For the exiting leader, prolonging the severance of relationships with staff can be painful. Continued 'check-ins' can undermine the new leader. It is best to leave and not return. Regardless, it is important that both leaders be gracious toward each other's point of view and work in a dignified manner. Public celebrations are a meaningful way to show unity, respect, and highlight the organization's accomplishments. Ultimately, the exiting leader wants to leave a legacy that is respected and good for the organization – particularly the staff, children, youth, and families. That legacy is influenced by the character displayed. Acknowledgement of common rituals that support professionals and sustain human and intellectual needs greatly reduce fear and chaos during a time of vulnerability for any organization.

TRANSITION PLAN

An effective transition plan describes the dimensions of leadership, charts a process, and explores ways for an organization to groom future leaders.

Recommended Reading

Bodilly, S. & Beckett, M. (2005). *Making Out-of-School Time Matter.* Santa Monica, CA: RAND Corporation.

Brafman, O. & Brafman, R. (2010). *Click: The Forces Behind How We Fully Engage with People, Work, and Everything We Do.* New York: Crown Publishing

Brinkman, R., & Kirschner, R. (2006). *Dealing with Difficult People: 24 Lessons for Bringing Out the Best in Everyone.* New York: McGraw-Hill.

Brock, A. & Hundley, H. (2016). *The Growth Mindset Coach: A Teacher's Month-by-Month Handbook for Empowering Students to Achieve.* Berkeley, CA: Ulysses Press.

Chester, E. (2012). *Reviving Work Ethic: A Leader's Guide to Ending Entitlement and Restoring Pride in the Emerging Workforce.* Austin, TX: Greenleaf Book Group Press.

Crenshaw, D. (2008). *The Myth of Multitasking: How Doing it All Gets Nothing Done.* San Francisco: Jossey-Bass.

Dweck, C. (2006). *Mindset: The New Psychology of Success.* New York: Random House.

Duckworth, A. (2016). *Grit: The Power of Passion and Perseverance.* New York: Scribner, Simon & Schuster.

Ericcson, A., & Pool, R. (2016). *Peak: Secrets from the New Science of Expertise.* New York: Houghton Mifflin Harcourt Publishing.

Fashola, O. (2002). *Building Effective Afterschool Programs.* Thousand Oaks, CA: Corwin Press.

Fletcher, A. (2007). *Lessons in Leadership: Words of Wisdom from Pioneer Directors Who Developed Exemplary Afterschool Programs:* Sacramento, CA: Center for Collaborative Solutions.

Gordon, J. (2007). *The Energy Bus: 10 Rules to Fuel Your Life, Work, and Team with Positive Energy.* Hoboken, NJ: John Wiley & Sons.

Halpern, R. (2006). *Critical Issues in After-School Programming.* Chicago: Erickson Institute.

Heifetz, R. & Linsky, M. (2002). *Leadership on the Line: Staying Alive Through the Dangers of Leading.* Boston: Harvard Business Press.

Holstein, W. (2008). *Manage the Media: Don't Let the Media Manage You.*

Boston: Harvard Business Press.

Howard, R. & Korver, C. (2008). *Ethics for the Real World: Creating a Personal Code to Guide Decisions in Work and Life*. Boston: Harvard Business Press.

Josephson, M. (2002). *Making Ethical Decisions*. Los Angeles: The Josephson Institute of Ethics.

King, L. (1994). *How to Talk to Anyone, Anywhere, Anytime: The Secrets of Good Communication*. New York: Three Rivers Press.

Kirschner, R. (2011). *How to Click with People: The Secret to Better Relationships in Business and in Life*. New York: Hyperion.

Kosmoski, G. & Pollack, D. (2000). *Managing Difficult, Frustrating, and Hostile Conversations*. Thousand Oaks, CA: Corwin Press.

Koulopoulos, T. & Keldson, D. (2014). *The Gen Z Effect*. Brookline, MA: Bibliomotion, Inc.

Lencioni, P. (2007). *The Three Signs of a Miserable Job*. San Francisco: Jossey-Bass.

Lencioni, P. (2016). *The Ideal Team Player*. San Francisco: Jossey-Bass.

National After School Association. (2009). *Code of Ethics: NAA*. Oakton, VA. https://naaweb.org/images/NAA-Code-of-Ethics-for-AferSchool-Professionals.pdf

Maraia, M. (2009). *Relationships Are Everything: Growing Your Business One Relationship at a Time*. Highlands Ranch, CO: Professional Services Publishing.

Maxwell, J. (2002). *Leadership 101: What Every Leader Needs to Know*. Nashville, TN: Thomas Nelson.

Maxwell, J. (2007). *Be a People Person: Effective Leadership Through Effective Relationships*. Colorado Springs, CO: David C. Cook

McKenna, C. (1998). *Powerful Communication Skills: How to Communicate with Confidence*. National Press Publication.

Miller, M. (2013). *The Heart of Leadership: Becoming a Leader People Want to Follow*. San Francisco: Berrett-Koehler Publishers.

Monarth, H. (2010). *Executive Presence: The Art of Commanding Respect Like a CEO*. New York: McGraw Hill.

Parker, D. (2003). *Confident Communication: Speaking Tips for Educators*. Thousand Oaks, CA: Corwin Press.

Price, A. (2004). *Ready to Lead? A Story for Leaders and Their Mentors*. San Francisco: Jossey-Bass.

Ricci, M. (2013). *Mindsets in the Classroom: Building a Culture of Success and Student Achievement in Schools.* Waco, TX; Prufrock Press.

Sanborn, M. (2006). *You Don't Need a Title to Be a Leader: How Anyone, Anywhere, Can Make a Positive Difference.* New York: Doubleday/Random House.

Santana, L., Rothstein, D. & Bain, A. (2016). *Partnering with Parents to Ask the Right Questions: A Powerful Strategy for Strengthening School-Family Partnerships.* Alexandria, VA: ASCD.

Seemiller, C. & Grace, M. (2016). *Generation Z Goes to College.* San Francisco: Jossey-Bass.

Simmons, A. (2007). *Whoever Tells the Best Story Wins: How to Use Your Own Stories to Communicate with Power and Impact.* New York: Amacon, American Management Association.

Smith, P. (2012). *Lead with a Story: The Guide to Crafting Business Narrat5ives That Captivate, Convince, and Inspire.* New York: Amacon, American Management Association.

Stillman, D. & Stillman, J. (2017) *Gen Z @ Work: How the Next Generation Is Transforming the Workforce.* New York: Harper Collins.

Strike, K. (2007). *Ethical Leadership in Schools.* Thousand Oaks, CA Corwin Press.

Strike, K. & Soltis, J. (2004). *The Ethics of Teaching.* New York: Teachers College Press.

Ulrich, D., Smallwood, N., & Sweetman, K. (2008). *The Leadership Code.* Boston: Harvard Business School Publishing.

Vollmer, J. (2010). *Schools Cannot Do It Alone: Building Public Support for American's Public Schools.* Fairfield, IA: Enlightenment Press.

Watkins, M. (2009). *Your Next Move: The Leader's Guide to Navigating Major Career Moves.* Boston: Harvard Business Press.

Weinstein, B. (2011). *Ethical Intelligence: Five Simple Rules for Leading a Better Life.* New York: MJF Books.

Whitaker, T (2015). *Dealing with Difficult Teachers.* New York: Routledge/Eye on Education.

Young, P. (2014). *Lead the Way!: 24 Lessons in Leadership for After School Program Directors.* (Lewisville, NC: ExtendED Notes/Gryphon House.

Young, P., Knight, D. & Sheets, J. (2005). *Mentoring Principals: Frameworks, Agendas, Tips, and Case Stories for Mentors and Mentees.* Thousand

Oaks, CA: Corwin Press.

Young, P. (2009). *Principal Matters: 101 Tips for Creating Collaborative Relationships Between After-School Programs and School Leaders.* Lewisville, NC: School Age Notes/Gryphon House.

Young, P. (2008). *Promoting Positive Behaviors: An Elementary Principal's Guide to Structuring the Learning Environment.* Thousand Oaks, CA: Corwin Press.

Young, P. (2018) *Teaching Grit and Mindset in Afterschool Programs: What Students, Staff, and Parents Should Know and Be Able to Do.* Columbia, SC: CreateSpace/An Amazon.com Company.

Index

Paul G. Young, Ph.D.

ABOUT THE AUTHOR

Dr. Paul G. Young, Ph.D., has worked as a high school band director, elementary and junior high classroom teacher (grades 4, 5, and 7), nearly 20 years as an elementary school principal, and as an executive director of an afterschool program, all near the area of Lancaster, Ohio. For more than 45 years he has also served as an adjunct professor of music classes at Ohio University-Lancaster campus. He holds a bachelor and master's degrees in music from the Ohio University School of Music. His doctorate, in Educational Administration, is also from Ohio University, Athens, Ohio.

He served in leadership roles with both the National Association of Elementary School Principals (NAESP) and the National AfterSchool Association (NAA). He was elected as president of the 30,000-member NAESP in 2002-2003. He served as a member of the NAA Board of Directors starting in 2008 before becoming NAA's President and CEO in 2010. He retired from association work in 2012. He has written extensively on the topic of school and afterschool alignment, led training workshops throughout the country, and played an influential role in the development of practical, evidence-based alignment strategies for school leaders and afterschool professionals. He is the author of several books for principals, music teachers, and afterschool professionals.

Dr. Young and his wife, Gertrude, a retired music teacher, live in Lancaster, Ohio. They have two adult daughters and sons-in-law. Katie and her husband Jon Steele live in Glendale, Wisconsin, where she is the principal oboist with the Milwaukee Symphony. She previously performed with the New World Symphony and the Florida Orchestra. Jon is the Field Marketing Director for the Eastern U.S. for Medshape, an Atlanta-based medical group. Mary Ellen and her husband Eric live in Glen Ellyn, Illinois. Mary Ellen is Senior Market Development Manager for McGraw Hill-Higher Education and Eric is a designer for Looney and Associates, Chicago.

Dr. and Mrs. Young enjoy their four grandchildren - Nora Rahn, Charles Steele, Evan Rahn, and Jonathan Paul "Jack" Steele and hope they each grow to enjoy a life filled with positive learning experiences – in school and after school.

Paul G. Young, Ph.D.

Other Books by Paul G. Young

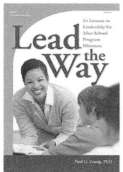

Lead the Way provides short, self-guided overviews that both aspiring and practicing after school professionals need to thrive in their roles. The 24 fundamental insights and strategies can be used as professional development topics with after school program staff, laying the foundation for the program to recruit, retain, and grown effective leaders. Highly popular content shared at National AfterSchool Association and state-affiliate conferences.

Despite the day-to-day accomplishments that every after-school program director and staff member enjoy, there often can be an equal number of challenges that after-school professionals face. One key to clearing these daily hurdles is by building bridges between your after-school program and the school principal. *Principal Matters* provides suggestions in 10 areas, including tips that enhance student learning, tips that support principal/program director collaboration, tips that develop advocacy for after-school programming and tips that support parent and community engagement. Whether you are new to the after-school field or a veteran, these 101 tips provide positive ideas that will lead to quality programs and positive relationships between after-school programs and school leaders.

Teaching Grit and Mindset in After School Programs is an easy-to-use, hands-on guide for understanding and teaching the success skills – grit and mindset – in the afterschool program environment. Are you working with kids your afterschool program who have potential but don't want to do anything? This is a commonsense resource for busy program leaders and their staffs who face the challenges of helping kids increase their perseverance and develop the mindset and motivation to complete homework and fully engage in out-of-school learning experiences. This book is packed full of ready-to-use professional development, resources, trips, vignettes, and instructional activities. It is organized in four parts, five chapters within each.

Made in the USA
Las Vegas, NV
10 September 2021

29985732R00069